GEORGE COME HOME

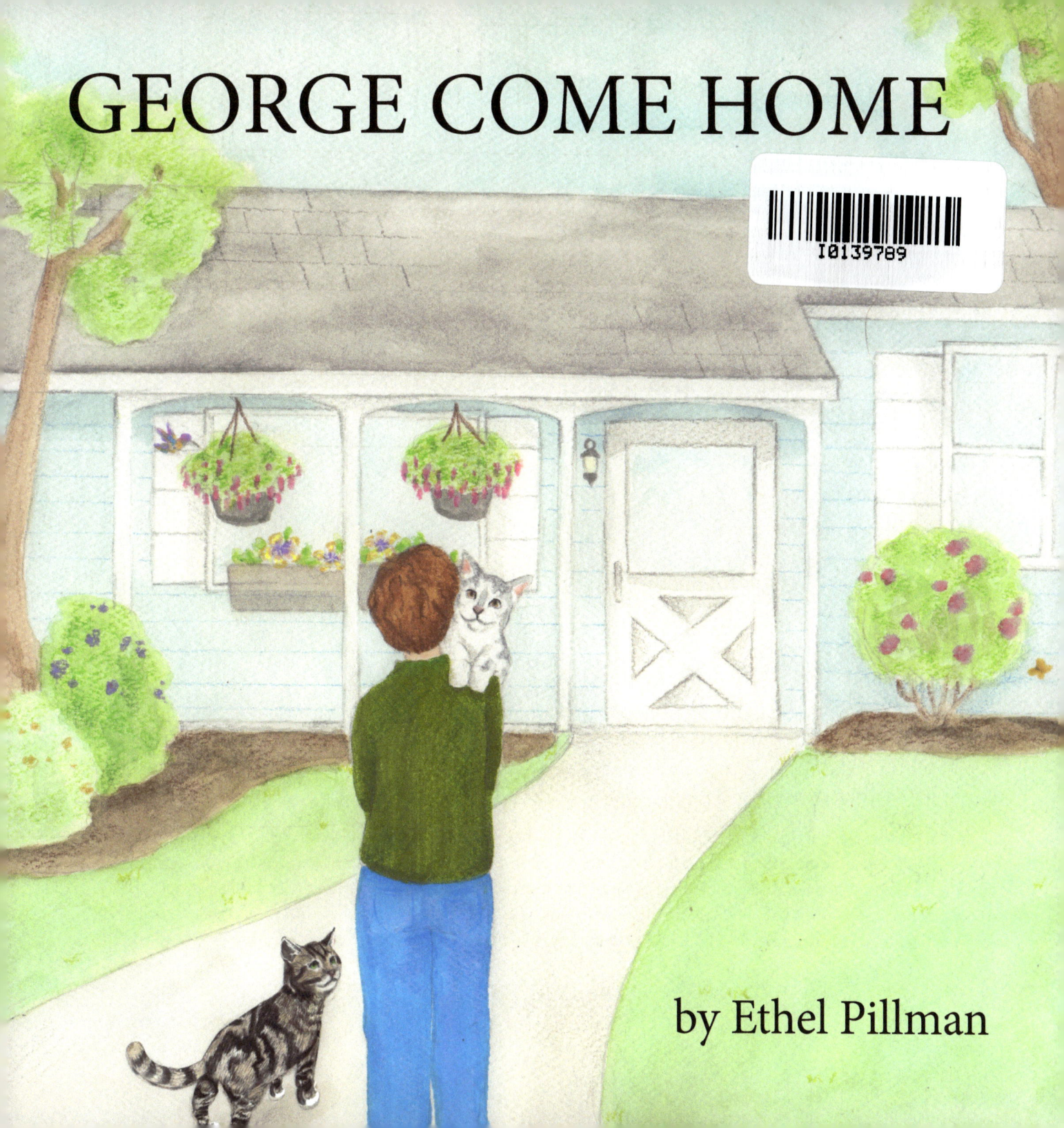

by Ethel Pillman

George Come Home

Ethel Pillman

Illustrations by Amelia DuMez

Illustration editing by David Neptune, Maria Noor, and Pavani Apsara

Copyright © Ethel Pillman 2025

Published by 1st World Publishing

P.O. Box 2211, Fairfield, Iowa 52556

tel: 641-209-5000 • fax: 866-440-5234

web: www.1stworldpublishing.com

First Edition

ISBN: 978-1-4218-3574-7

LCCN: Library of Congress Cataloging-in-Publication Data

This book is dedicated to…

Erin and Michael

The Ihlenfelds

And to West Bend, Wisconsin ~
the place I'll always call home

A very special thank you to my daughter, Erin Pillman,
who worked tirelessly to edit this book,
and also to facilitate the publishing process.

Thank you also to our wonderful publisher Rodney Charles of
1st World Publishing.

Without you two, the manuscript for this book would probably be buried
somewhere in George's litter box.

Based on a true story.

There once was a cat named George.

He knew that he was a very special cat.

He was mostly grey, with white fur on his chest.

He thought he looked like he was wearing a grey tuxedo with a white shirt.

He also thought that he was very handsome and very smart.

George lived with his human friend, Mom, and his cat friend, Reilly.

They lived in an ordinary house.

George and Reilly had ordinary toys, and ate ordinary food.

But George knew that he was not ordinary.

He knew that if he were human, he would be the president,
a king, or a famous movie star.

George loved to run outside with his friend Reilly.

They lived near Lake Michigan where they liked to fish.

George also liked to roll in the dirt in Mom's beautiful flower garden. That made his "white shirt" turn brown, but he didn't mind because he was good at cleaning himself.

Mom's neighbors knew and loved George and Reilly.

One of the neighbors, Mary, gave them tasty treats when they visited her.

Another neighbor, Ruth, always left a bowl of food for them on her porch.

George and Reilly also liked to run and play in the nearby forest
with their friends.

They would play all afternoon, until dinnertime.

After dinner they would play with their toys.

They went to bed early because they were so tired after their busy day.

George and Reilly snuggled together in their little bed and slept soundly.

One evening, Reilly came home, but George didn't. Mom asked Reilly if he had seen George, but Reilly hadn't because he had been cat napping all afternoon. Mom asked Mary and the other neighbors if they had seen George. They all said, "No." They wondered where he could be.

Mom called the animal shelter to see if someone had found him and taken him there, but the people there hadn't seen him.

Because they knew that George was very handsome, they thought that maybe he had found a girlfriend.

Since George sometimes visited the city, Mom called all of her friends there, but they hadn't seen him either.

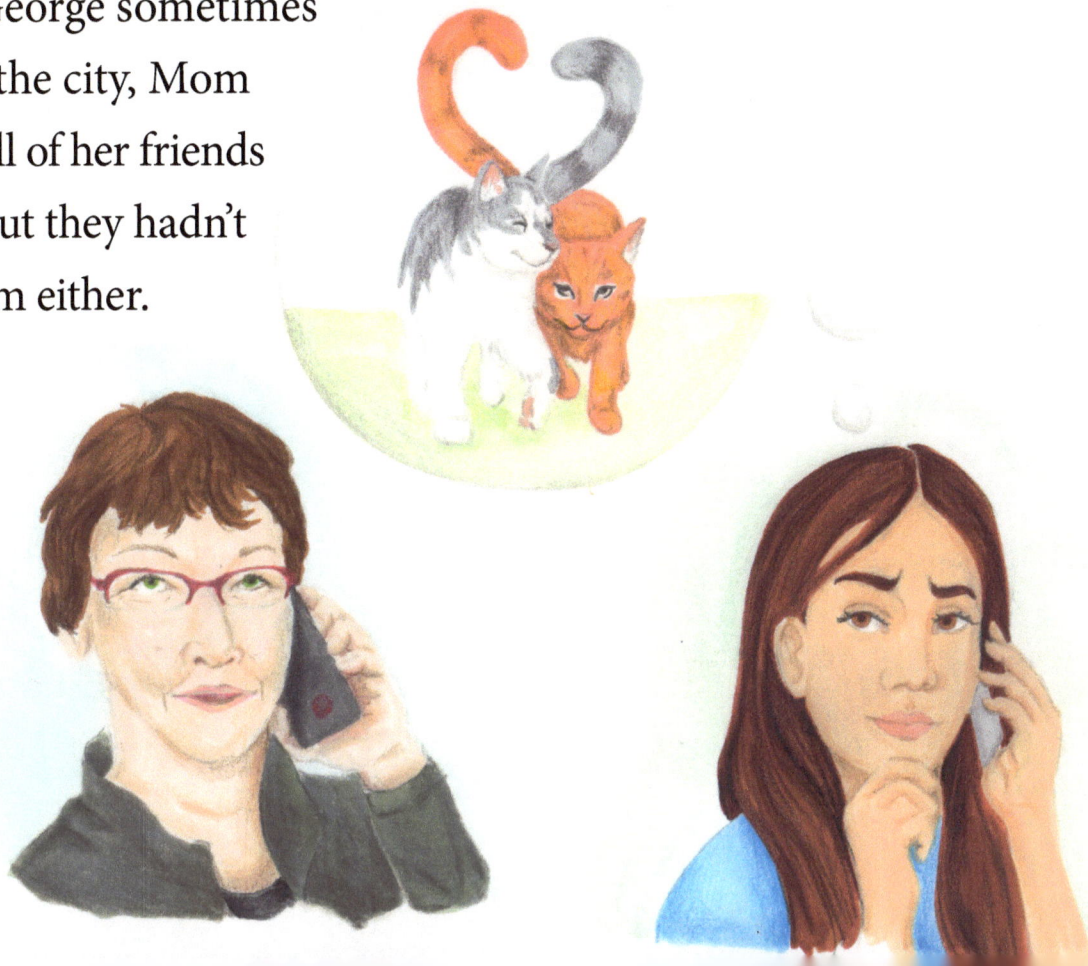

Reilly and Mom thought that maybe George had forgotten to come home because he was having so much fun with his forest friends.

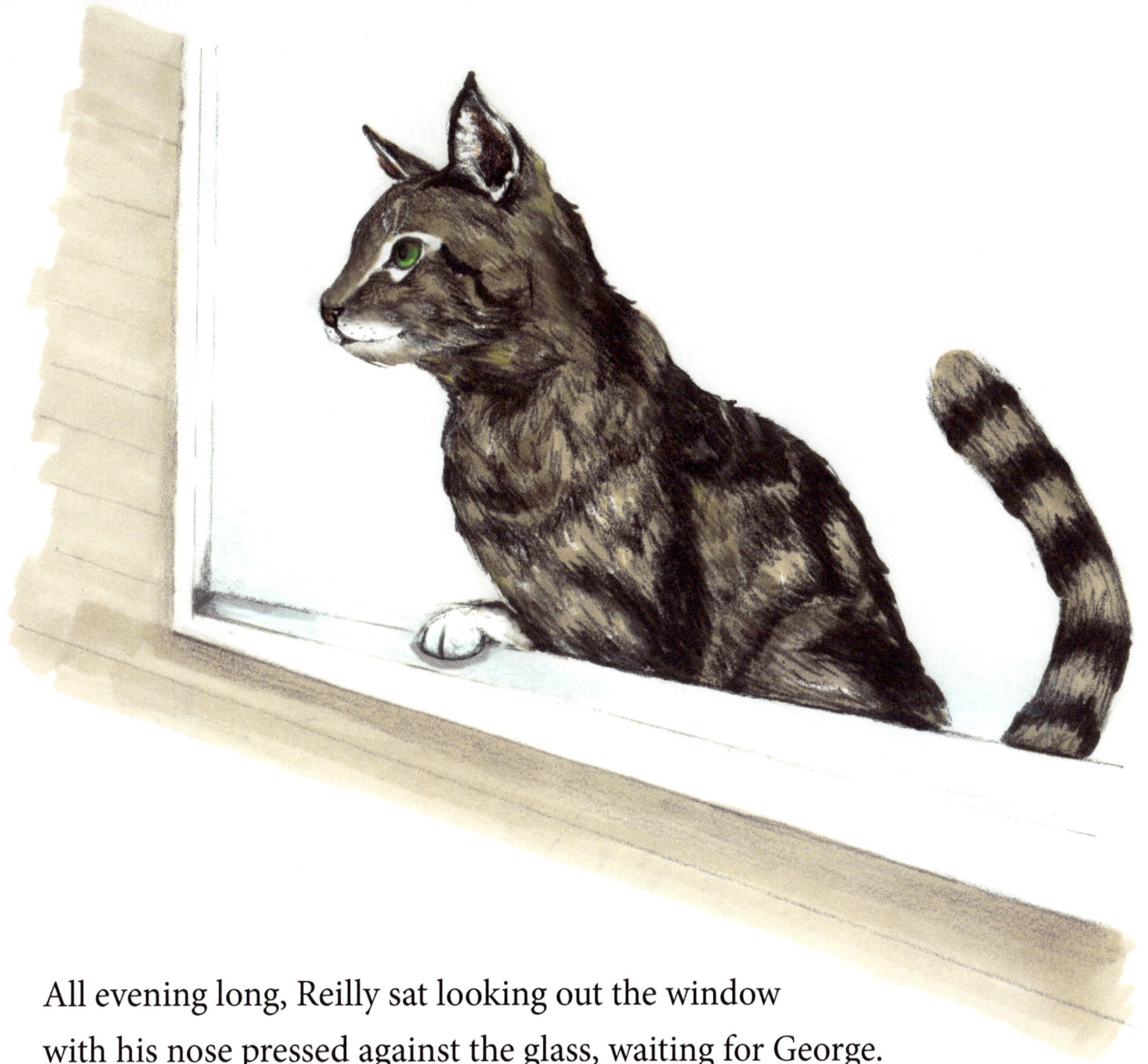

All evening long, Reilly sat looking out the window
with his nose pressed against the glass, waiting for George.

Finally they went to bed, hoping that George would be back in the morning.

But when they woke up, George was still missing. And they felt sad. Mom wondered if George had decided to live in a tree house. So she and Reilly went to the forest to look for him, but he wasn't there.

Then they drove around the neighborhood in Mom's car.

They rolled down the windows and called his name.

"George! George!"

MISSING

IF YOU SEE GEORGE
PLEASE CALL
452-6006
HIS FAMILY MISSES HIM

As time went on, Mom and Reilly began to wonder if they would ever see their friend George again.

They decided to make posters and hung them around the neighborhood.

Now we will find out George's story.

The day began just like any other day.

Reilly and George went fishing in the morning. George caught two tiny silver fish, and Reilly caught one.

Reilly was tired, so he went home for a nap while George played with his forest friends all afternoon.

When he got hungry, George decided to go home.

Just then, a woman walked up to him and said, "Oh, sweet kitty, you must be lost.

My name is Lulu.

You can come live with me."

Of course he wasn't lost! He had lived here for many years! All the other neighbors knew him, but Lulu didn't because she was new to the neighborhood. She spoke to George very sweetly and offered him some tasty treats, just like Mary did. As he started to eat the treats, she picked him up and carried him into her house.

Lulu was not ordinary. She wore fancy clothes. Her house was much nicer than Mom's house. She knew how special he was, and treated him like a prince. She even called him "Prince" and gave him a little crown to wear.

Unlike his house, where he ate the same food every day, Lulu brought George large platters of fresh fish. And she gave him lots of new toys. George was finally living like the royal cat he always knew he was! George thought about how jealous Reilly would be if he knew that George was living in such a grand place.

George meowed at the door to let Lulu know that he wanted to go outside.

She told him that he had to stay inside so he wouldn't get lost again.

He hadn't been lost, but he didn't know how to tell her.

After a while, George got tired of the fancy food and new toys. He even knocked the crown off his head. He no longer wanted to be at Lulu's house. He wanted to be in his ordinary house with Mom and Reilly again. And he missed his forest friends.

George looked out the window and saw his house,
but didn't know how to ask Lulu to take him home.
He wanted to escape, but how could he do it? He needed a plan.

One day, Lulu left to go shopping,
and George went to the basement.
There he met Mack the Mouse.

Mack asked George who he was. George told Mack his story.
Mack told him that Lulu didn't know that Mack was living
down there. And Mack said he would try to help George.

Suddenly, George had an idea! He had a feeling that Lulu was probably afraid of mice, and he knew just what to do.

This is how George thought the plan would work.

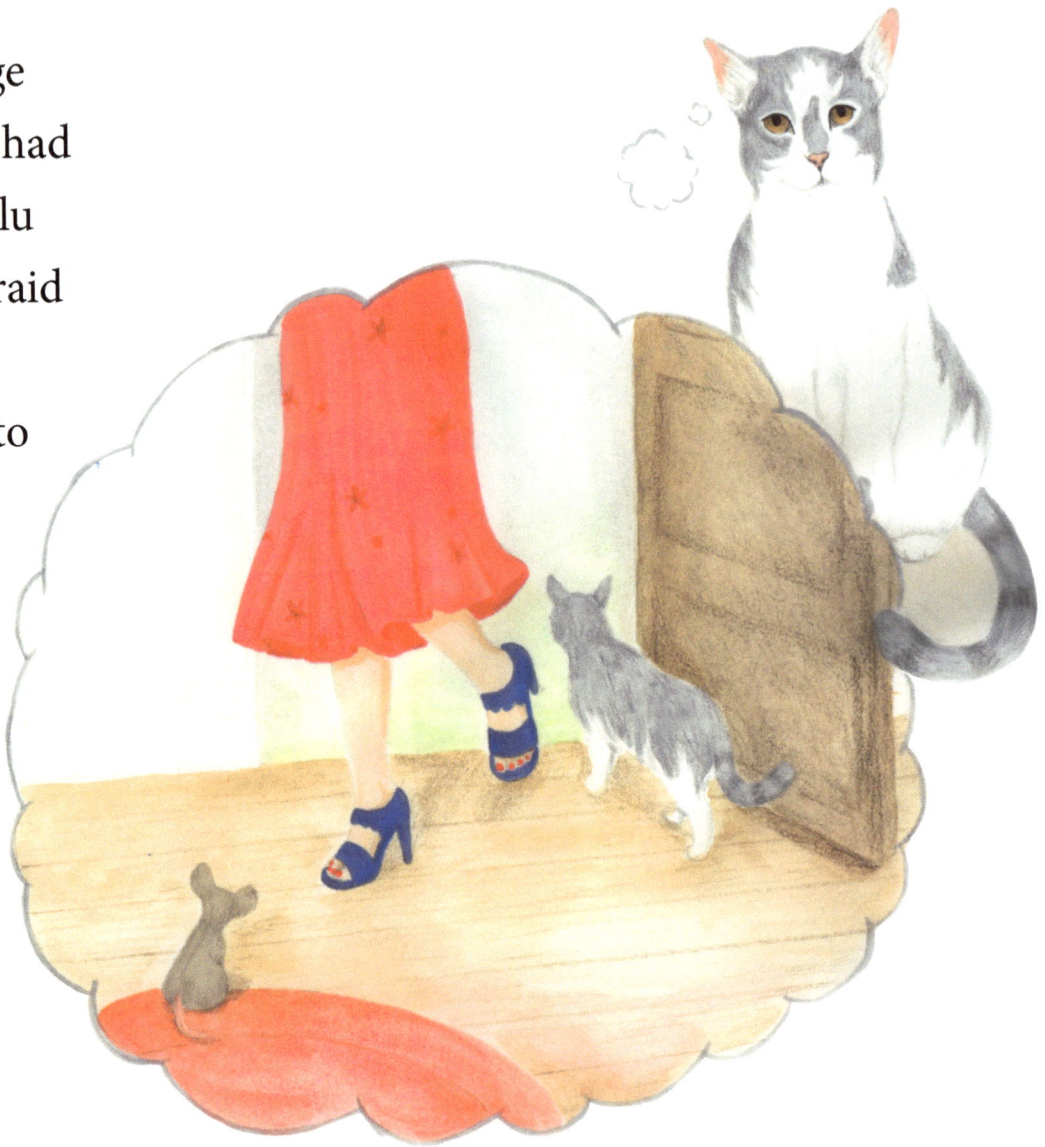

Lulu would come home. Mack would be sitting inside the door when it opened. She would see Mack. She would scream and be so upset than she would forget that the door was open. And then George would run to his house as fast as he could.

This is what really happened. Mack and George saw Lulu's car drive up. Mack sat by the door, as Lulu opened it. She said, "Oh, you cute little mouse! How did you get in here? Let me get you something to eat." She didn't want Mack to leave, so she quickly closed the door.

So they needed a new plan. The next day, Lulu left again. George saw a fireplace with a chimney. He thought that he could get inside the chimney and climb all the way to the top. Then he would jump to the roof, jump down to the ground, and run home.

But once George got inside the fireplace and started climbing,
he realized that it wasn't as easy as he had thought it would be.
The walls were slippery, and he soon fell back down to the bottom.

He was very dirty from all the black chimney soot.
And he was also very disappointed.

Just then the door opened. Lulu walked in and saw George.

"Oh my! What happened to you? You need a bath!"

She didn't know that cats do not like water.

The only baths they want are the ones they give themselves.

Lulu put George in the bathtub with bubble bath! He jumped out and ran away, getting dirty water on the white carpet in the living room.

George needed a new plan, but he was
out of ideas.

Sometimes he could see Mom walking by,
and he could hear her calling his name.

"George! George!" He meowed to let her
know where he was, but she couldn't hear him.

One day he saw Mom and Reilly drive by calling
for him, so George wrote "SOS" on the window
with Lulu's bright red lipstick. They still didn't see
him.

Later that day, Lulu came into the house with a poster, and George's picture was on it. He was so excited! He thought that she would call Mom, and he would finally get to go home.

MISSING

But Lulu put the poster on the table and left it there for days. She didn't call because she liked having George live with her.

Then one day Lulu saw
George looking at the poster.
Tears were running down his
face and dripping from his
whiskers.

George knew that
Lulu wanted him
to stay with her
because he was
so special, but he
wanted to go home.

When Lulu saw how sad George was, she
knew that she had to make the phone call.
Even though Lulu was going to miss him,
she knew that it was the right thing to do.

Slowly, she picked up her phone and called the number on the poster.

A few minutes later, Mom and Reilly rang the doorbell.

Mom thanked Lulu and said that George and

Reilly could visit her anytime.

And then Mom carried George home in her arms.

That night Mom had a party to celebrate. She invited the whole neighborhood. The neighbors got to meet Lulu, and everyone told George they were glad to see him again.

George was happy to be home. It had never felt so good to be there with Mom and Reilly and his toys. George loved his family and home more than ever, and felt very special in his ordinary house.

The author and her inspiration.

Ethel Pillman lives in Sheboygan, Wisconsin.

She has two grown children, Erin and Michael.

She currently works at Mead Public Library. After 40 years of working as a registered nurse, she decided it would be fun to do something new. And she had always loved books and appreciated the important role of the library in the community.

She wrote this book after her cat George went missing for four days and was found living at a neighbor's house. It was a happy reunion when he returned home.

When Ethel isn't writing she can be found working in her award winning flower gardens, enjoying walks along the shores of Lake Michigan, playing sheepshead, or playing practical jokes on her friends.

And she hopes you enjoy this book as much as she enjoyed writing it.

www.ingramcontent.com/pod-product-compliance
Lightning Source LLC
Chambersburg PA
CBHW041427090426
42741CB00002B/71

9 781421 835747